CAREER
BOT
Use ChatGPT to
Easily Find Your Next Job
JOB HUNTING IN THE AGE OF AI
Sugar Gay Isber McMillan

Career Bot: Use ChatGPT to Easily Find Your Next Job

Published by **The WOW Book Co.™**
Austin, Texas, USA
www.TheWOWBookCo.com

ISBN **978-1-967973-72-9**
Large Print Edition

Printed in the United States of America

Library of Congress Control Number: [Leave blank or enter once assigned]

For permissions, media, or collaboration inquiries, contact: info@TheWOWBookCo.com

Table of Contents

How to Use ChatGPT - Your Tool, Not Your Boss

You don't need to be a tech expert to talk to your bot. You just need curiosity and a few simple habits.

This page gives you the basics for how to get the most from ChatGPT or any AI assistant.

---

1. Choose How You'll Talk

You can talk to ChatGPT in several ways:

- **Typing:** The simplest. Type your question or paste in text and read the reply.

- **Voice Mode:** Tap the **headphone or mic icon** to speak naturally. You can pause, mumble, or trail off—ChatGPT won't interrupt you.

- **Dictation:** On desktop or mobile, press your device's microphone button (Windows key + H on PC, or built-in mic on phone) to speak instead of typing.

- Remember, it can and will make mistakes; check your work.
- 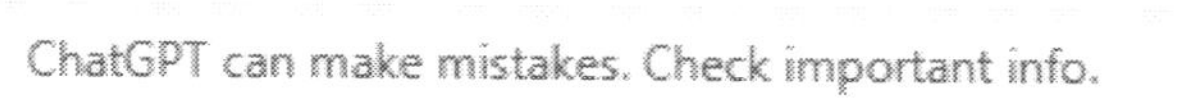

---

2. Add Files and Context

You can share what you're working on so ChatGPT can help:

- **Attach a File:** Click the "+" **icon or paperclip** to upload a PDF, Word document, spreadsheet, or image.
- **Paste Text:** Copy text from your résumé, cover letter, or email and paste it directly into the chat box.

- **Give Clear Instructions:** Tell ChatGPT exactly what you need, e.g.,

"Please edit this résumé for clarity and format it for a marketing manager role."

---

3. Use Follow-Up Prompts

Conversation is where the magic happens. Try:

- "Give me three options."
- "Make that sound more professional."
- "Summarize this for a recruiter."
- "Turn this into a 30-second elevator pitch."

Each response teaches your bot how to help you better.

---

4. Save, Copy, and Reuse

When you like what ChatGPT creates, **copy and paste** it into a Word or Google Doc.

You can also use the **Share or Export** buttons to save conversations for later reference.

---

5. Protect Your Privacy

Never share your home address, Social Security number or any confidential work data.

Use ChatGPT as a *thinking partner,* not a filing cabinet.

---

6. Stay Kind and Curious

Politeness improves prompts - and perspective.

End each session by thanking your bot for its help, even if it sounds silly. It reminds you that *you're human* and that gratitude keeps technology in its rightful place: as a tool for good.

INTRODUCTION | Here We Go

If you've never been fired, you're a rare person.

Fired, let go, laid off - whatever you call it - it's still the end of a job.
And that in-between time, the *unknown*, can be terrifying.

What am I going to do next?
How will I pay my bills?
What if nothing comes along?

That free fall is real. Losing a job ranks right up there with moving or getting divorced - three of life's most stressful experiences.

I get it.

Right now, I'm coming to the end of a four-year contract that isn't being renewed. I've been told, and I've gone through every stage of grief: denial, bargaining, hope, frustration and finally, acceptance. I've got one month left.

So, I wrote this book for both of us.
Because in the four years since I last looked for a job, everything has changed.

The Old Way

Updating a résumé and cover letter used to take *days*.
You'd rewrite, reformat, and rethink everything - again and again.

I remember an old trick people swore by: copy the job description, paste it at the bottom of your résumé in a one-point white font, and hope the computer scanners picked it up.

That was the era of trying to *beat the robots.*

The New Way

Now, we *work with them.*

Here's what I do today:
I copy and paste a job description directly into ChatGPT.

Then I click the little + to attach my résumé.
And I say,

"Please update my résumé so it closely matches this job description."

In seconds - bam - it's done.
All the clutter disappears. My old résumé was a monument to every year and every achievement. The new one is lean, focused, and relevant.

And yes, I talk nicely to my bot.
Always say *please* and *thank you.* Being human still matters - even to the machine.

If something feels missing, I adjust it.
If I want to add a key project, I do.

The point is: this is the new workflow of 2025.
You hand over the mechanics of the search to

your chatbot - your research assistant, résumé editor, motivational coach and skill sampler - all rolled into one.

Why I Wrote This

Because I'm standing where you are right now - thinking about my next paycheck, my next role and my next chapter.

I know the anxiety of watching time run out. I also know the relief of realizing I'm not powerless.

Working with ChatGPT has changed how I look for work and how I think about myself in that process.

It's faster, calmer and strangely hopeful.

I've written fifteen books about working with bots, but this one is different.

This one is about *starting over.*

Let's Do This Together

Follow along.

Talk to your bot.

Let it write, rewrite, and re-energize you.

ChatGPT - and every tool like it - is going to be as essential as a smartphone once was. At first, it feels awkward. Then it becomes second nature. Soon, you'll wonder how you ever did without it.

So wherever you are in your job search - fired, laid off, waiting, or worrying - welcome.

This book is your guide to staying calm, clear, and employable in an AI-driven world.

Let's go down this road together.

May it bring you clarity, confidence, and, most of all, a job that fits the life you want next.

CHAPTER 1 | MEET YOUR NEW RECRUITER

You're not imagining it - work has changed. Not the hours, not the effort, but the *feel*.
What used to be satisfying now feels mechanical, measured in metrics instead of meaning.

You send résumés into portals that never reply.
You complete projects no one sees.
You're busy every minute and invisible all the same.

Whether you're hunting for a job or hanging on to one, you've felt it: the slow erosion of purpose.

Author Patrick Lencioni calls it *the three signs of a miserable job* - **irrelevance, immeasurability, and anonymity.**

You can't see how your work matters, you can't tell if you're improving, and no one seems to notice either way.

That's not failure; it's fallout. The modern workplace is optimized for efficiency, not for people.

But here's the twist: the same technology that stripped the humanity out of work can now help you reclaim it.

Career Bot isn't another app to manage you. It's a mindset - and a toolkit - for taking back control of your working life.

It's a way to turn artificial intelligence into *actual intelligence* about yourself: what you're good at, what you value, and where you want to go next.

This book is for three kinds of readers:

1. The laid-off or job-hunting professional trying to stay hopeful.
2. The overworked employee stuck in the "busy but bored" cycle.
3. The mid-career pivot-seeker who wants a map, not more noise.

You'll build your own digital assistant - a **Job Scout Bot** - that can:

- Scan job sites for roles that truly match your experience and goals.
- Filter by salary, location, or work-style preference.
- Tailor your résumé and cover letter in minutes.
- Track responses so nothing slips through the cracks.
- Free your brain for the parts of work that still require a human touch.

Think of it as hiring an assistant who never sleeps, never complains, and never forgets what you asked for.

And the best part? You don't have to be a technical expert. If you can write an email, you can build your own bot.

Before we begin, take a moment to reflect on your current situation.

Field Exercise 1: Your Work Story

Open a new page in your notebook or document and write three short statements.

1. **What do I do now?**
2. **What makes me feel invisible at work?**
3. **What kind of work would make me feel seen again?**

You won't share this with anyone. It's your private benchmark. Every tool you build in this book will point back to these three answers.

Mission Brief

You're going to learn how to:

- Build a Job Scout Bot in under fifteen minutes.
- Re-write your résumé and cover letters to sound alive again.
- Discover what kind of work actually matches who you are now.

This isn't about replacing you with a machine. It's about *refusing to feel replaceable.*

Next up: Chapter 2 | Build Your Job Scout in 15 Minutes
We'll set up your first working ChatGPT Agent, teach it what to look for, and turn the job hunt - or the hunt for meaning - back in your favor.

CHAPTER 2 | BUILD YOUR JOB SCOUT IN 15 MINUTES

"If you're going to walk into a storm, bring an umbrella.
Or better yet, bring a bot."

You don't need a computer science degree to build your first AI helper.
You need a story, a clear goal, and fifteen focused minutes.

1 | Why You Need a Scout

When I first built my own Career Bot, I was sitting at the same desk where I'd been for years at a global tech company.

I wasn't fired, but I wasn't seen either.
So I decided to see what the machines could see.

Within an afternoon, my new "assistant" had:

- Collected ten open roles that actually matched my résumé.

- Flagged companies expanding in my city.
- Summarized each job description into a one-sentence "fit" statement.

That was the moment I realized: I didn't need *motivation*, I needed *automation*.

---

2 | Gather Your Tools

Before you start, have these nearby:

- A computer or tablet with ChatGPT Plus (for custom GPT access).
- A recent copy of your résumé.
- A short paragraph describing the kind of work you want.
- Your coffee, tea, or whatever courage tastes like today.

Optional but helpful: a folder where you'll store everything this bot finds.

---

3 | Set Your Mission

Every bot starts with a mission statement. Think of it like briefing a new employee on Day 1.

Example:

"You are my personal Job Scout Bot. Search the web each morning for mid-level instructional design or technical writing jobs in Texas that pay over $80,000, remote or hybrid preferred. Present your top 10 finds in a short list with links and company summaries."

Write yours now. Keep it short, specific, and measurable.
(Tip: The more detail you give, the smarter it behaves.)

---

4 | Create Your Custom GPT

Step-by-step walkthrough:

1. Open ChatGPT > Explore GPTs > "Create a GPT."
2. In the "Instructions" field, paste your mission statement.

3. Add follow-up instructions:
    - "Summarize listings into three bullet points."
    - "Highlight company culture keywords."
    - "Ignore ads older than 14 days."
4. Upload your résumé if the interface allows - this helps it match skills.
5. Name your agent something human: *Scout*, *Radar*, *Maven TX* - whatever makes you smile.

Press Save. You now have an assistant who works while you sleep.

---

5 | Ask Your Scout to Run a Test Search

Type a simple prompt:

"Find 10 current technical writing positions in Texas that fit my résumé."

Your Scout will:

- Search across job boards and company pages.
- Filter duplicates and expired listings.
- Return a short, clean report with links.

Pro Move: ask it to *rank* results by match strength or cultural fit.

If you're mid-career and looking for something new, you can add:

"Include roles that use my skills in education, training, or creative writing."

In seconds, you have a curated briefing instead of a rabbit hole.

---

6 | Make It Personal

Your Job Scout gets smarter when you talk to it. Try these follow-ups:

- "Remove companies with less than 100 employees."
- "Add any positions with flexible schedules."

- "Tell me which of these roles are growing industries."

Each tweak trains your agent to think more like you.

---

7 | Keep Score

Every week, ask your Scout:

"How many new roles did you find? Which ones overlap?"

Copy those results into a simple tracker or spreadsheet.
Columns: Date | Company | Role | Link | Status (Interested / Applied / Interview).

This makes progress visible - a cure for that "nothing's happening" feeling that kills motivation.

---

8 | Field Test – Mini Mission

Objective: teach your bot nuance.
Ask it:

"Search for jobs that use creativity and writing but are *not* marketing."

See what it delivers. Discuss results like a mentor:

"Why did you include this one?"
"What keywords triggered that match?"

Every correction is a training moment.

---

9 | Celebrate the Small Win

Your first successful search is proof: you're not powerless.
You just needed the right kind of help.
You now have a digital teammate that never gets tired of looking out for you.

Take a screenshot. Name the file *CareerBot_Day1.pdf.*
That's your first milestone.

Mission Checklist

- Mission statement written

- Custom GPT created and tested
- Résumés uploaded or summarized
- Tracker started
- First 10 roles found

If all boxes are ticked, congratulations - you've built your first operational Career Bot.

Next Up | Chapter 3 Resume Reframe

We'll teach your new assistant to polish, rewrite, and target your résumé so it finally gets read by humans - and the machines standing guard in front of them.

CHAPTER 3 | RESUME REFRAME

"Your résumé is not a biography.
It's a flashlight - point it where you want to go."

1 | The Problem with the Paper Trail

The modern résumé was built for a world that no longer exists.

In a digital maze of automated systems, it's less a ticket to a job than a passport that needs the right stamps to get through the gate.

I work at one of the world's largest technology firms, which I will not name in this book. I watched talented people vanish into the ATS void. Their résumés were beautiful, but unreadable by machines. They would tell me that after they were let go or left, finding a job was impossible.

I knew the reason:
No keywords. No measurable results. Just paragraphs of effort disguised as experience.

The good news: ChatGPT - and soon, your own **Career Bot** - can help you rebuild your résumé as a *living document*, one that speaks to both humans *and* algorithms.

---

2 | Understand the Gatekeeper

Most companies use an **Applicant Tracking System (ATS)** that:

- Scans for exact keyword matches.
- Ranks applications based on frequency and placement of those words.
- Filters out any résumé that can't be parsed.

That's why people say, "robots are rejecting you."

They aren't judging your worth - they just can't *read* you.

---

3 | Feed Your Career Bot the Raw Material

Before you can rewrite, gather:

- Your most recent résumé (even if outdated).
- A list of three roles you'd love to land.
- Job descriptions for those roles (copy the text).
- A quick note describing your proudest results - numbers, projects, outcomes.

Upload or paste all of this into your Career Bot and say:

"Analyze these job descriptions and highlight the top recurring keywords and required skills. Then compare them to my résumé and list what I'm missing."

You'll get a gap report within seconds.
That's your upgrade list.

---

4 | Rewrite with Purpose

Now tell your bot:

"Rewrite my résumé to reflect these skills and metrics while keeping my authentic tone. Prioritize clarity and measurable results. Use action verbs."

Pro Tips:

- Limit bullet points under each job to 4–6.
- Start each with a *result*, not a duty.
    - Instead of *"Responsible for training staff,"* write *"Trained 12 technicians, cutting onboarding time by 30%."*
- Save a "master résumé" with everything, and a short version per role.

---

5 | Style for Both Humans and Machines

Formatting rules that matter:

- Use a clean font (Arial, Calibri, Helvetica).
- Avoid tables, text boxes, and graphics that ATS can't read.
- Keep section headers simple: *Experience, Skills, Education, Awards.*
- Export as **.docx** or **.pdf (text-based)**, never as an image.

When in doubt, ask:

"Career Bot, check if this résumé is ATS-friendly."

It will flag layout issues before a recruiter ever sees them.

---

6 | Add the "Proof of Life" Section

One of Lencioni's three miseries was **anonymity**.
Combat it right on the page.
Add a small final section titled **"Selected Highlights"** or **"Impact Snapshots."**

Bullet ideas:

- Mentored three new hires who now lead projects of their own.
- Launched an internal guide still used company-wide.
- Collaborated across six time zones without missing a deadline.

This is where you sound human again.

---

7 | Let Your Bot Compare Versions

Ask:

"Compare this résumé to the job posting for [Company Name]. Suggest edits to raise my match score to 90%."

Your assistant will tweak wording, re-order bullets, and surface the right phrasing.
You still approve every change - AI drafts, *you decide.*

---

8 | Field Exercise – The 30-Minute Makeover

1. Paste your current résumé into Career Bot.
2. Choose one dream job listing.
3. Run the "compare and rewrite" sequence.
4. Paste the new version back into Word and skim it aloud.
5. Circle any line that doesn't sound like you and edit it.

That's your first pass. It doesn't need perfection - it needs progress.

Mission Checklist

- Résumé uploaded and analyzed
- Keywords list created
- Revised version drafted
- ATS check completed
- Human "voice" proofread

Next Up | CHAPTER 4 | Cover Letters That Sound Human

Because a résumé gets you noticed, but a cover letter gets you *remembered.*

CHAPTER 4 | COVER LETTERS THAT SOUND HUMAN

"A résumé shows what you've done.
A cover letter shows who you are."

1 | Why Cover Letters Still Matter

When recruiters skim hundreds of résumés, they're not looking for perfection - they're listening for a *voice*.

That one paragraph that makes them stop and think, *I'd like to work with this person.*

AI has flooded inboxes with copy-and-paste templates.

The result? Everything sounds the same. That's why a genuine, specific letter - crafted with your **Career Bot** but guided by *you* - stands out more than ever.

---

2 | Start with a Story, Not a Salutation

Forget "Dear Hiring Manager."
Open with something that only *you* could say:

"Last year I helped a team of five launch a system used by 40,000 customers.
Now I'm looking for a role where I can keep solving big, messy problems."

Stories give context. Details build trust.
Humans remember *people*, not bullet points.

---

3 | Brief Your Bot Before It Writes

Feed your Career Bot these ingredients:

- The exact job posting text.
- Your current résumé.
- A short note describing why you want the job (one or two sentences).
- Any metrics or results that show success.

Then prompt it with:

"Draft a 250-word cover letter in my natural tone.
Focus on curiosity, collaboration, and measurable outcomes."

---

4 | Polish the First Line Until It Sparkles

Your first sentence is your handshake.
Aim for *warm and specific*, not gimmicky.

Try:

- "When I read your posting for a project manager who thrives in organized chaos, I smiled - that's my natural habitat."
- "Your company's focus on renewable design reminded me why I became an engineer."

Avoid:

- "I am writing to apply for..."
- "Please accept my résumé for consideration..."

---

5 | Structure That Works Every Time

1. **Hook** – one personal line or mini-story.
2. **Bridge** – how your skills connect to the role.
3. **Proof** – one quantified result.
4. **Fit** – why you and this company align.
5. **Close** – a confident, grateful sign-off.

Example closing:

"Thank you for the opportunity to apply. I'd love to bring the same focus and energy that helped my last team cut production time by 25%."

---

6 | Let Your Bot Be Your Editor, Not Your Voice

After you draft:

"Career Bot, review this letter for clarity and flow.
Keep my personal tone; fix grammar and rhythm only."

Then read it out loud. If it doesn't sound like you talking to a real person over coffee, rewrite it until it does.

---

7 | Field Exercise – Two Letters, One Day

1. Choose two different job listings.
2. Paste each into Career Bot and run the same prompt.
3. Compare the drafts.
4. Highlight phrases that sound *too polished* or *too generic* - that's the AI showing.
5. Replace those lines with a sentence from your own voice.

You'll start hearing the difference between "AI formal" and "you confident."

Mission Checklist

- Job description analyzed
- 250-word draft created

- First line rewritten for impact
- Personal story added
- Final version read aloud

Next Up | CHAPTER 5 | THE HIDDEN JOB MARKET

We'll explore where the real opportunities hide - and teach your Career Bot how to find them before they hit the job boards.

CHAPTER 5 | THE HIDDEN JOB MARKET

"Half the jobs you see aren't real.
Half the real jobs you never see."

1 | The Myth of the Open Listing

Every day, millions of people apply for positions that were already filled, frozen, or written just to satisfy HR policy.
The visible job market - what you scroll through on LinkedIn or Indeed - is only about **20 percent** of what's actually available.

The rest lives underground: referrals, internal moves, contracts quietly extended.

Your **Career Bot** is your lantern in that dark maze.
It can't guarantee a shortcut, but it can show you where the paths really lead.

---

2 | Why the Gig Economy Isn't Freedom

The gig boom promised independence:
work anywhere, set your own hours, escape the office.
But here's what most influencers don't post between airport lounges and latte shots:

- **Unstable income.** Platforms change algorithms overnight; "good months" vanish.
- **No safety net.** Benefits, healthcare, and retirement plans disappear.
- **Isolation.** Freelancers trade bosses for silence.
- **Constant self-promotion.** Every gig is another audition.
- **Burnout disguised as freedom.** When your brand *is* your job, you're never off-duty.

The truth: the gig economy works beautifully for the platforms - not always for the people powering them.

Field Note

A digital-nomad photographer once told me she spent more time negotiating Wi-Fi than taking photos.
The pictures looked effortless; the life behind them wasn't.

---

3 | Behind the Highlight Reel

Scroll any social feed and you'll see the same dream: the smiling traveler with a laptop on a beach.
But look closer - there's glare on that screen, sand in the keyboard, and a deadline off camera.

Those who succeed as global freelancers usually have:

- A specialized skill set (coding, design, consulting).
- A backup savings cushion.
- A strong professional network.

- Reliable clients before they board the plane.

Without those, “freedom” quickly becomes financial turbulence.

---

4 | What the Hidden Market Really Looks Like

The good work - the kind that sustains people - is exchanged quietly through:

- **Internal referrals.** Employees recommend people they trust.
- **Contract extensions.** Short-term roles that quietly become permanent.
- **Professional associations.** Communities where people trade leads long before public listings appear.
- **Small-business networks.** Vendors, clients, and former colleagues passing names.

To tap that flow, you need two things: *visibility* and *credibility.*
AI can help you build both.

---

5 | Train Your Bot to Hunt Below the Surface

Prompt examples:

"Find companies in Austin expanding technical-writing teams but not yet advertising roles."
"List startups that recently raised Series A funding in sustainable tech."
"Summarize five people on LinkedIn who changed jobs at [Company Name] this quarter."

Each query uncovers signals that hiring may be coming soon.
Add those leads to your **Career Tracker** spreadsheet - your growing personal map of the hidden market.

---

6 | Networking Without the Awkwardness

Let your bot help you start genuine conversations, not sales pitches.

Ask:

"Draft a short outreach message to a project manager at [Company X] who recently posted about onboarding challenges."

Send that with a simple line: *"Saw your post - really insightful. I've worked on similar issues, happy to share ideas."*

That's it.

You're now in the conversation that lives under the job board.

---

7 | When a Gig Becomes a Gateway

Not all freelance work is failure. Some gigs open doors to long-term partnerships.
The trick is to **choose gigs that teach, not just pay.**

Ask before accepting:

- Will this add proof of skill I can showcase?
- Does it connect me with people in my target industry?
- Could it evolve into a retainer or staff role?

If the answer is yes to even one, it's not a side hustle - it's a stepping-stone.

---

8 | Field Exercise – Your Underground Map

1. Pick three companies you'd love to work for.
2. Ask your Career Bot:

"Find 10 people who recently joined or left these companies. Summarize their job titles."

3. Note patterns: growth areas, new departments, recent funding.
4. Send two authentic connection messages this week.

You're not applying; you're *appearing.* That's how people find you before positions ever post.

Mission Checklist

- Gig-economy myths understood
- First hidden-market search run
- Outreach templates tested
- Underground map started

CHAPTER 6 | INTERVIEW TRAINING WITH AI

"The first person you have to convince you can do the job is yourself."

1 | Why Talking Out Loud Matters

Most of us type our thoughts.
But careers are built - and won - in conversation.

Typing to a bot feels safe; talking to it feels strange - until you realize it's rehearsal for the real thing.

When you speak, your brain organizes ideas differently.

You discover where you stumble, what you repeat, and what you actually believe.

That's why **Voice Mode** isn't a gimmick - it's practice with feedback.

---

2 | Setting Up Voice Mode

If you can say "Hey Google" or "Alexa," you can talk to your **Career Bot**.

On Mobile (iOS / Android):

- Open the ChatGPT app.
- Tap the 🎧 icon (bottom-right).
- Choose a voice and grant microphone access.
- Start speaking naturally - pauses and "uhh" included.

On Desktop:

- Click the microphone icon in the chat bar.
- Allow browser microphone access.
- Speak normally; you can interrupt your bot and it will keep up.

Your bot won't cut you off mid-sentence or lose the thread.

It listens the way a good interviewer should.

---

3 | Warm-Up Drill – The Out-Loud Résumé

1. Open Voice Mode.
2. Say:

"Career Bot, ask me to walk through my résumé as if you're a recruiter."

3. Answer in full sentences.
4. When you finish, ask:

"Summarize how confident I sounded and which answers felt weak."

You'll get instant notes on pacing, tone, and clarity - coaching that costs nothing but honesty.

---

4 | Field Note – The Hardest Question

Every interview begins the same way:

"So ... tell me about yourself."

It sounds simple, but it's the hardest question in the room.

Most people panic, then list job titles in chronological order.

That's not what the interviewer wants.
They're listening for *story*, *motivation*, and *energy*.

Think of your answer as a **90-second origin story** - why you chose this path and what keeps you curious.

Leave out family details or dates that could reveal your age.

Focus on purpose and momentum.

Example frame:

"I've always been drawn to storytelling, which led me to study journalism.

I didn't realize then how writing would connect every part of my career - from books and social media to technical communication and education.

What I've learned is that clear writing isn't just a job skill; it's how people build trust.

That's what makes me excited about this role."

Short. Warm. Memorable.

Voice Mode Drill:

"Career Bot, ask me the interview question 'Tell me about yourself.' After I answer, tell me what felt engaging and what sounded rushed."

Repeat until your story sounds natural - like you're talking to a friend who genuinely wants to know.

5 | Behavioral Questions Without the Freeze

Interviewers love the "Tell me about a time when …" format.
Use your bot to rehearse with the **STAR method** - Situation, Task, Action, Result.

Prompt:

"Ask me five behavioral questions for a customer-service role. After each answer, critique how clearly, I described the result."

Then refine:

"Help me tighten each story to under 90 seconds."

Talking out loud trains timing, not just wording.

6 | Voice Mode as Your Confidence Coach

Voice Mode isn't just about answers - it's about rhythm and reassurance.
Try these:

- "Career Bot, ask me ten quick icebreakers."
- "Interrupt me mid-answer so I can practice staying calm."
- "Rate my tone from 1 to 10 for warmth and authority."

Five minutes a day is enough to retrain your voice for clarity and confidence.

---

7 | The Mock Interview Blueprint

1. Paste a real job description into chat.
2. Say:

"Conduct a 15-minute mock interview for this role. Alternate technical and behavioral questions."

3. Answer out loud.
4. End with:

"Summarize my top three strengths and weaknesses from this session."

Save the transcript - it becomes your personalized prep guide.

---

8 | Advanced Prompt Ideas

- "Simulate an interview with a skeptical manager."
- "Ask me curveball questions about company culture."
- "Pause after each question so I can practice controlling filler words."
- "Evaluate whether my examples show measurable results."

---

9 | Field Exercise – Talk Yourself into Calm

Before bed, open Voice Mode and say:

"Career Bot, ask me why I'm good at what I do."

Speak for two minutes - no script, no notes.
Tomorrow, play it back.
That's your baseline for confidence.

● Reality Check – What NOT to Talk About or Show in an Interview

Print this list and read it before every call or meeting. It will save you from avoidable mistakes.

Topics to Avoid Entirely

1. **Family or Caregiving Details** – Keep the focus on your skills, not your household.
2. **Medical, Dental, or Financial Issues** – No mention of illnesses or bills.
3. **Politics or Religion** – Neutral background and conversation only.
4. **Age Clues** – Skip high-school stories and graduation dates. Keep examples within the past 10 years.
    - If asked, deflect with: > "I've kept learning throughout my career and bring that energy to every role."

5. **Questions They Can't Ask** – Age, marital status, sexuality, religion, ethnicity, or family plans. If asked, pivot:

"I'd love to focus on how I can contribute to this position."

6. **Past-Employer Complaints** – Replace grievances with lessons.
7. **Compensation – Not Yet** – Discuss money only after a written offer.

Appearance and Presentation

Every interview - whether across a desk or a screen - is a two-minute visual audit before a single question is asked.

Before You Arrive (or Log In)

- Turn off your phone completely.
- Brush your teeth, comb your hair, and clean your nails.
- Light fragrance only; aim for fresh, not noticeable.

- Avoid all-black outfits - choose navy, charcoal, or medium gray.
- Bring only essentials: résumé folder, pen, briefcase or purse. No coffee cups, water bottles, or snacks.
- Check your background if it's a video call - simple, tidy, no political symbols.

During the Interview

- Camera at eye level; shoulders and face visible. Put your laptop or camera on a box or several boxes so you are not looking down or up during the interview.
- Light facing you, not behind you. Lighting is so important. Adjust your camera's settings to make sure you look your best.
- Wear make-up and dress like you would if you were meeting the company HR team.
- Sit forward slightly; arms uncrossed.
- Maintain a natural smile and steady eye contact.

- Use the interviewer's name at least twice.
- Ask curious questions about their work and listen to the answers.

Why It Matters

Interviewing is largely a process of elimination. Show up clean, calm, and courteous and you've already cleared half the field.

Mission Checklist

- Voice Mode tested
- Résumé walk-through practiced
- Behavioral answers rehearsed
- Mock interview completed
- Appearance and etiquette reviewed

Quick Reference Sheet | Interview Training with AI

"You can't fake calm. But you can practice it."

Chat Prompts to Practice with Your Career Bot

- "Ask me five common interview questions and rate my clarity."
- "Simulate a behavioral interview using the STAR method."
- "Interrupt me mid-answer so I can learn to recover gracefully."
- "Role-play a skeptical interviewer and help me respond with confidence."
- "Summarize my tone and pacing - was I too fast, too flat, or just right?"

The Warm-Up Routine

1. **Voice Mode on.**
   Talk, don't type. It builds rhythm and trust in your own voice.

2. **Record, replay, refine.**
   You'll hear where you hesitate and where you shine.
3. **Stand up.**
   Body language affects tone - even over audio.
4. **Smile.**
   It changes how you sound, literally.
5. **Stop at ten minutes.**
   Interview practice works best short and daily, not marathon-style.

What to Prepare

- **Three stories** showing leadership, problem-solving, and teamwork.
- **One failure** story that ends in growth.
- **Two insightful questions** to ask every interviewer.

- **A 90-second "Tell me about yourself"** summary you can deliver anywhere.

Mindset Reminders

- *You're not auditioning for perfection – you're demonstrating self-awareness.*
- *If you forget a question, pause. It shows composure, not weakness.*
- *Interviews aren't tests. They're partnerships in progress.*

Ask your Career Bot:

"Give me one interview confidence quote every morning this week."

Next Up | CHAPTER 7 | SALARY AND NEGOTIATION SCRIPTS

Your Career Bot has helped you find roles and nail interviews.

Next, it will help you navigate the moment that makes everyone nervous - discussing money.

CHAPTER 7 | SALARY AND NEGOTIATION SCRIPTS

"If you don't name your worth, someone else will - and they'll round down."

1 | Why We Freeze When Money Comes Up

Money is the one topic everyone cares about and no one prepares for.
You can talk easily about strategy, teamwork, leadership - but when the interviewer says, *"So, what are your salary expectations?"* most people stammer or give a number too low.

It's not greed that causes hesitation. It's conditioning. We've been taught that talking about money is rude.
But silence isn't polite; it's expensive.

Your **Career Bot** will help you practice that conversation until it feels as natural as any other business topic.

---

2 | When to Talk About Money

Never before there's an offer.
Until then, you're gathering data, showing fit, and building interest.

If pressed early, say:

"I'm sure we can find a range that works once we've determined if it's a good mutual fit."

If they insist:

"Based on similar roles in this industry and region, I'd expect somewhere around $____ to $____, depending on the overall package."

That phrase "overall package" buys you time and flexibility.

"The first offer is rarely the best offer. It's an invitation to start the real conversation."

---

3 | Know Your Range Before They Ask

Use your Career Bot to research:

- Typical salary bands for your title and location.
- Cost-of-living differences if remote.

- Benefits that carry cash value - insurance, bonuses, stock, time off.

Prompt:

"Find salary ranges for mid-level instructional designers in Texas, and summarize the total-compensation factors that usually add 10–15 percent to base pay."

Make note of the numbers in your tracker spreadsheet. Knowing the facts keeps nerves from taking over.

"Negotiation isn't conflict; it's collaboration about value."

---

4 | Rehearse the Conversation

Use Voice Mode again for realism.

Prompt:

"Career Bot, play the role of a hiring manager making me an offer.
Quote a number 10 percent below my target and challenge me to respond professionally."

Then practice:

"Thank you - I appreciate the offer. I was hoping for something closer to $____ based on [skills/results].
Is there room to adjust the base or overall package?"

Repeat until it sounds confident but kind.

---

5 | The Power of the Pause

Once you make your counteroffer - stop talking.
Let the silence work for you.

Negotiators call it *the golden pause.*
You've said your value; now give them space to respect it.

"Confidence doesn't come from the number on the paycheck. It comes from knowing you can ask for it."

---

6 | If You Hear "No"

A “no” isn’t the end; it’s data.
Ask, calmly:

“I understand. Could you share the constraints around the number?”

Then pivot:

“Would there be flexibility in signing bonus, vacation, or professional-development support?”

Companies often have soft budgets in one area when another is capped.

---

7 | Negotiation Scripts for Common Situations

Scenario 1 | The Range Question Too Early

“I’m still learning about the role’s responsibilities.
May I share a range once I understand the expectations fully?”

Scenario 2 | Offer Below Market

"I appreciate the offer. Based on my research, similar roles are around $____.
Is there room to align closer to that?"

Scenario 3 | Multiple Offers

"I'm fortunate to have another opportunity in a similar range, but I'm more excited about your mission.
If we can meet at $____, I'd love to move forward quickly."

Scenario 4 | They Ask What You're Making Now

"My current compensation reflects a different scope of work.
I'm focused on ensuring this next step reflects the responsibilities we've discussed."

"They wouldn't be interviewing you if they couldn't afford you."

---

8 | Field Exercise – Your Negotiation Blueprint

1. Use your Career Bot to pull three real job listings in your field.

2. Research their pay range with public data.
3. Write a short negotiation script for each.
4. Record yourself in Voice Mode reading them aloud until you can say each one without flinching.

Save those scripts - they become your muscle memory for every future offer.

---

9 | Mindset for the Money Talk

Negotiation isn't about squeezing; it's about **aligning value.**
You're not asking for charity - you're calibrating fairness.

Remember:

- You are interviewing them too.
- The way a company handles this conversation tells you everything about its culture.
- If they pressure or shame you for asking, that's not a red flag - it's a stop sign.

3 ½ | Research Tools for Real Numbers

Before you ever quote a figure, collect real data from credible salary-tracking sites.

Each has a slightly different focus - together they give a fuller picture of what the role is actually worth.

Start with these:

- **Glassdoor .com** – Employee-reported salaries and reviews; use filters for title, company size, and city.
- **PayScale .com** – Compares pay by years of experience, certifications, and education.
- **Salary .com** – Traditional HR-sourced data with cost-of-living adjustments.
- **Indeed Salaries (indeed.com/salaries)** – Aggregates listings to show active-market pay, not just historic averages.

- **LinkedIn Salary** – Shows median pay by region and role for users who share compensation data.

Then ask your **Career Bot** to cross-analyze what you find:

"Compare salary data from Glassdoor, PayScale, and LinkedIn for [job title] in [city, state].
Summarize the low, mid, and high ranges and note which benefits are most often included."

Remember that **location matters.**

A salary that feels solid in Des Moines might barely cover rent in Portland or New York. Use your bot to factor in cost-of-living differences before you settle on a number.

"Negotiation isn't conflict; it's collaboration about value."

Mission Checklist

- Salary research completed
- Negotiation prompts practiced in Voice Mode
- Counteroffer phrasing rehearsed
- Alternate benefits identified
- Confidence restored

Next Up | CHAPTER 8 | RE-SKILL, RE-BRAND, RE-LAUNCH

You've learned to name your worth.
Now it's time to expand it - using AI to sharpen skills, rebuild your professional brand, and relaunch your career on your own terms.

CHAPTER 8 | RE-SKILL, RE-BRAND, RE-LAUNCH

"Every career stalls eventually. The smart ones rebuild before anyone notices."

1 | Why Reinvention Isn't Optional

Careers don't die; they drift.
The trick is catching yourself before drift becomes doubt.

Technology, markets, and entire job categories now change faster than job titles.
Learning something new every year isn't optional anymore - it's survival.

The good news? You already have a 24-hour research assistant who never gets bored of teaching you.

---

2 | Audit Your Current Skill Set

Start with an honest inventory.
Ask your Career Bot:

"List my top ten transferable skills based on my résumé and note which are at risk of automation in the next five years."

Then run:

"Identify three complementary skills that would future-proof my career."

Common upgrade paths:

- Customer service ↠ user-experience design
- Administration ↠ project coordination
- Writing ↠ content strategy or instructional design
- Retail ↠ supply-chain analytics

Highlight one area that excites you; that's your re-skill target.

---

3 | Find the Shortest Learning Path

You don't need a second degree - you need momentum.

Prompt examples:

"Career Bot, find reputable free or low-cost online courses for [data analysis / UX / digital marketing].
Summarize time commitment and certification value."

Reliable platforms:

- **Coursera** – University-partnered certificates
- **edX** – Harvard / MIT consortium
- **LinkedIn Learning** – Short professional refreshers
- **Google Certificates** – Highly employable in tech support, analytics, UX
- **Khan Academy** – Math / finance refreshers

Block 30 minutes a day. Consistency beats intensity.

"If you wait to feel ready, you'll wait forever."

---

4 | Re-Brand Your Digital Presence

Once your skills shift, your story must too. Begin with LinkedIn - the hiring world's first impression.

Checklist:

- Update headline with *function + focus* ("Instructional Designer | Learning Experience Architect").
- Replace your old headshot with a clear, current image.
- Rewrite your summary in the first person; keep it under 150 words.
- Add new certifications and remove outdated software.
- Post one short insight each week from something you're learning.

Ask your Career Bot:

"Rewrite my LinkedIn About section to reflect my new skills while keeping my authentic tone."

"Your résumé gets you an interview; your reputation gets you invited back."

---

4 ½ | Protect Your Digital Reputation

"They'll Google you before they greet you."

Every hiring manager runs a thorough background search.
Your name, your photos, your posts - everything you've ever liked or shared - forms a first impression before you speak a word.

If your online footprint feels casual or chaotic, clean it before you apply anywhere.

Email Matters

- Retire the fun address from college. *hotRoxy@rocketmail* or *guitarhero69@aol* sends the wrong message.

- Create a neutral, professional address that uses your name: firstname.lastname@gmail.com.
- **Use this address only for job searches and career correspondence.**

Social Media Reality Check

- Assume every recruiter will search for your name on Google, Instagram, TikTok, Facebook, and LinkedIn.
- Review the first two pages of results - that's what they'll see.
- Delete or archive anything that could raise questions: arguments, political rants, off-color humor, heavy partying.
- If you want a private space, make your accounts invite-only or use an alias not tied to your legal name.
- Avoid posting about your current job, coworkers, or grievances - companies monitor those, too.
- Remember: screenshots live forever.

"Privacy settings aren't paranoia; they're armor."

The Smart Social Strategy

- **Keep one public, professional presence (LinkedIn or a portfolio page) that reflects your brand.**
- **Keep your personal accounts locked and separate.**
- **Before each job search, Google yourself again. If something unflattering appears, bury it by posting new, relevant, positive content.**
- **Ask your Career Bot:**

"Audit my online presence for anything that could harm a job search. Suggest ways to improve professional visibility."

The Goal

To make sure what shows up first online

supports what you say in person.
When your résumé, LinkedIn, and digital trail all tell the same story, you look organized, trustworthy, and ready.

"Your online trail is your modern résumé - even the parts you didn't mean to write."

---

5 | Build a Portfolio - Even If You're Not a Designer

Proof beats promises.
Every field has artifacts that show competence:

Career Type	What to Showcase
Writer	Blog posts, guides, internal docs
Trainer	Slide decks, lesson plans
Marketer	Campaign snapshots, metrics
Engineer	GitHub repos, prototypes
Manager	Case studies, project retrospectives

Create a simple site (Notion, Google Sites, or Wix).

Your Career Bot can draft blurbs and organize layout copy.

---

6 | Re-Launch Quietly

Don't announce "Looking for Work" right away. Instead, let your activity tell the story.

Steps:

1. Follow ten companies in your target field.
2. Comment thoughtfully on two posts a week.
3. Publish one article or update monthly.
4. Join a virtual meetup or local workshop once a quarter.

Momentum attracts momentum.

"Opportunity rarely knocks twice - but it follows noise."

---

7 | Field Exercise – Your 30-Day Re-Launch Plan

1. **Week 1:** Skill audit + choose learning path
2. **Week 2:** Enroll + update LinkedIn headline
3. **Week 3:** Create one portfolio sample
4. **Week 4:** Reach out to three new connections and share progress

Log results in your Career Tracker. Small wins compound fast.

Mission Checklist

- Skill audit completed
- Online course enrolled
- LinkedIn updated
- Portfolio sample published
- 30-Day Plan set

Next Up | CHAPTER 9 | ADVANCED TACTICS FOR EXECUTIVES

You've refreshed your skills and story.
Now we'll look higher up the ladder - how mid- and senior-level professionals can use AI to craft a *Unique Value Proposition* and unlock the hidden executive job market.

CHAPTER 9 | ADVANCED TACTICS FOR EXECUTIVES

"If you've built a career of results, don't start begging for relevance. Redefine it."

1 | The Executive Identity Crisis

For many leaders, the problem isn't skill - it's visibility.
You've spent years building systems, teams, and brands. Now those same systems run without you.
AI, flattening org charts, and budget cuts have made "senior" feel like a warning label.

You're not obsolete. You're just between versions.
This chapter is about rewriting the executive playbook for an economy that now rewards adaptability over authority.

---

2 | Reclaim the Narrative

Executives often become ghosts in their own story.
Your title and company once spoke for you, but now *you* have to speak for yourself.

Ask your Career Bot:

"Rewrite my professional summary as a personal mission statement that positions me as a strategist, not a survivor."

Then replace every "I managed" with "I built," "I created," or "I changed."
Action verbs show leadership better than titles.

"Authority doesn't live in a job title. It lives in your verbs."

---

3 | Craft a Unique Value Proposition (UVP)

Hiring at the top is about solving pain points. A great UVP tells a board or CEO, *"I solve this specific kind of chaos."*

Use this 3-line format:

1. **Who you help:** "I help organizations struggling with..."
2. **What you deliver:** "I specialize in..."
3. **Why it works:** "By combining [experience + approach], I create measurable results."

Prompt example:

"Career Bot, help me write a UVP that positions me as a turnaround strategist for tech firms undergoing AI transition."

Once you have it, weave that line into your résumé header, LinkedIn bio, and every interview.

---

4 | Rebuild Your Strategic Network

Executives rarely get jobs through job boards; they get them through trust.
That means *relationships first, résumés second.*

Steps to restart your network:

- Reconnect with 10 trusted peers and former team members.
- Ask them what their companies are struggling with.
- Share one insight or solution - not a résumé, not a request.
- Follow up a week later.

"Your next opportunity won't come from your network. It'll come from your *reputation* inside it."

Your Career Bot can help:

"Draft three reintroduction messages for professional contacts I haven't spoken with in a year."

Keep tone light, curious, and generous.

---

5 | Navigate the Hidden Executive Job Market

Roughly **80 percent** of executive roles are never posted publicly.
They move through headhunters, retained search firms, and private referrals.

Ask your Career Bot to compile:

"A list of reputable executive-search firms in my industry and region, including contact submission links."

Then prepare a one-page **Leadership Portfolio** with:

- Short bio and headshot
- Core achievements with metrics
- UVP statement
- Sample press quotes or published thought pieces

It's your digital handshake for private searches.

---

6 | Publish, Speak, Mentor

Visibility rebuilds credibility.

Start small:

- Write one short article on LinkedIn each month.
- Offer to mentor younger professionals through alumni networks.
- Record a 3-minute video sharing a leadership lesson you've learned.

"If people can't see you teaching, they'll assume you stopped learning."

Mentorship also keeps you connected to emerging trends - your best defense against being quietly phased out.

---

7 | AI for Executive Reinvention

Executives who thrive in the next decade will be those who *partner* with AI instead of fearing it.

Prompts to explore:

- "Analyze my past projects and identify leadership skills AI can't replicate."
- "Summarize how to communicate human value in an automated workplace."
- "Draft a workshop outline titled 'Leading with AI Empathy.'"

Experimenting with AI tools signals relevance - and confidence.

---

8 | Field Exercise – The 90-Day Executive Relaunch

Week 1–2: Define your UVP and update all bios
Week 3–4: Contact 10 peers and 3 search firms
Month 2: Publish one article or recorded insight
Month 3: Present or mentor once, online or in person

Log each action in your Career Tracker. Small visibility steps compound faster than big announcements.

Mission Checklist

- UVP written and visible
- Leadership Portfolio created
- Key contacts re-engaged
- Article or talk published
- 90-Day Relaunch Plan in motion

CHAPTER 10 | THE QUIET EXIT: WHEN WORK LETS YOU GO WITHOUT SAYING IT

"Not every layoff comes with a meeting invite. Sometimes they just stop calling your name."

1 | What Quiet Firing Looks Like

Quiet firing - also called *constructive dismissal* or *quiet cutting* - is when a company decides you're finished but doesn't want the headline. Instead of pink slips, you get silence.

Common signs:

- You're excluded from meetings or group chats that once mattered.
- Your projects vanish or get reassigned.
- Your manager cancels one-on-ones and stops giving feedback.
- Raises, promotions, or conference invites disappear.
- HR goes radio-silent.

You haven't changed; the company's priorities have.
And they'd rather you take the hint than the severance.

"Neglect is a form of communication. You just have to be fluent in what it's saying."

---

2 | Why It Happens

Quiet firing is the corporate version of ghosting.
Leaders want to cut costs without morale fallout or legal exposure.
They reduce your relevance until you either burn out or resign.

Other quiet trends orbit it:

- **Quiet Cutting:** Restructuring you sideways into a dead-end role.
- **Quiet Cracking:** Staying "fine" while you're breaking inside.
- **Loud Quitting:** The backlash - public frustration when silence fails.

None of these are about personal failure. They're about organizations avoiding accountability.

---

3 | Recognize It Early

The sooner you spot the pattern, the sooner you regain control.

Watch for:

- Sudden drop in communication frequency.
- Your calendar empties while others' fill.
- Feedback shifts from coaching to compliance.
- Colleagues whisper, "I thought you were still on that project?"

Document what changes and when. Patterns matter if you ever need to prove constructive dismissal.

"Clarity is protection. Write down what vanishes."

4 | What to Do Next

1. **Stop waiting for validation.** You may never get closure.
2. **Secure your references** before they drift away.
3. **Update your portfolio and résumé immediately.**
4. **Reconnect with allies outside your current chain of command.**
5. **Engage your Career Bot:**

"Create a re-launch plan for someone experiencing quiet firing, including exit-strategy prompts and mental-reset steps."

If the job is slipping away, don't cling - *pivot.* Leaving on your own terms beats being erased slowly.

5 | When to Stay and When to Go

Ask three questions:

1. Am I still learning here?
2. Am I still respected here?
3. Am I still visible here?

If the answer to two or more is *no*, the job has already ended.
You're just finishing the paperwork in slow motion.

"You can't resurrect relevance in a place that's already written you out of the story."

---

6 | Reclaim Your Voice

Quiet firing takes your narrative and replaces it with absence.
Re-branding, networking, and re-launching are how you steal it back.
Post your wins, share your insights, speak at events.
Silence is the company's tactic - don't make it your habit.

---

7 | Unlocking the Hidden Job Market

"The best jobs aren't posted. They're proposed."

Roughly **80% of all open positions are never advertised.**
They exist in conversations, referrals, or the quiet moments when a company realizes they have a problem and no one yet assigned to solve it.
These are the opportunities that belong to people who *reach out first.*

When your visibility fades - or when you've been quietly fired - your next move is not to refresh a job board. It's to re-enter that unlisted market.

How to Access It

1. Identify five companies you admire and could genuinely help.
2. Research their current challenges (press releases, investor calls, or LinkedIn posts).

3. Use your **Unique Value Proposition (UVP)** as the anchor:

"I help [company type] solve [specific problem] by [unique method]."

4. Reach out to a decision-maker directly with a *Value Letter.*

The Value Letter - Your Secret Weapon

A **Value Letter** is not a résumé or cover letter. It's a short, one-page document written like a mini business proposal that answers a single question:

"If you hired me, what value would I bring immediately?"

Structure of a Value Letter

1. **Header:** Your name and contact info
2. **Intro:** Two sentences about the company's current challenge

"I saw your announcement about expanding into renewable packaging. That's an exciting move."

3. **Insight:** Identify what's likely missing or difficult

"One challenge companies face in that transition is balancing sustainability with reliable supply chains."

4. **Solution:** Show what you can do

"In my previous role, I led a cross-functional team that improved vendor sustainability ratings by 37% while reducing costs 12%. I'd love to help you achieve similar results."

5. **Close:** Invite a conversation, not a job

"If this aligns with your goals, I'd welcome a brief call to exchange ideas."

Short, specific, and centered on *them*, not *you.* That's what makes it magnetic.

Ask your Career Bot:

"Draft a Value Letter for a company facing [specific issue], using my résumé as context."

"A résumé lists the past. A Value Letter starts the future."

Why This Works

- It bypasses **Applicant Tracking Systems** that screen for keywords instead of people.
- It reaches decision-makers before HR filters intervene.
- It turns you from *an applicant into an advisor.*

The Value Letter isn't begging for employment; it's *offering help.*

That single shift - problem-solver instead of job-seeker - is how people re-enter the workforce with confidence after being quietly cut out of it.

"If they don't post the job, create it."

Mission Checklist

- Quiet-firing signs identified
- Timeline of events documented
- References confirmed
- Exit plan drafted with Career Bot

The Network Effect: Who You Know Still Matters

"Algorithms don't hire people. People hire people."

Behind every online job listing is a conversation that already started without you. That's why **networking** - real, human, face-to-face connection - is still the most reliable path to employment.

Up to **70–80% of jobs are filled through referrals**.

Sometimes it's as simple as *knowing someone who knows someone* who's hiring.

And sometimes, it's about timing: being visible when a manager thinks, *"Who do I know that could do this?"*

Inside the Referral System

Many companies pay **referral bonuses** when employees bring in a successful hire.

These range from $100 to $500 - or several thousand for hard-to-fill roles.

That means your contacts have an incentive to refer you.

Don't hesitate to ask:

"If your company has an employee-referral program, would you mind submitting my résumé?"

You're not asking for a favor.

You're helping them earn a bonus *and* fill a need.

"Opportunity doesn't knock; it whispers through introductions."

How to Activate Your Network

- **Update your LinkedIn profile** and toggle "Open to Work."
  Add the green banner - recruiters really do filter for it.

- **Reach out privately** to ten people you've worked with, studied with, or volunteered beside.
  Tell them what kind of role you're looking for.

- **Ask for warm introductions, not jobs.**
  "If you hear of someone who needs X, would you connect us?"

- **Attend networking events and civic groups.**
  Rotary Clubs, professional meetups, or city business dinners often lead to genuine referrals.

- **Follow up once a month** with updates on your progress - visibility keeps the opportunity alive.

Your **Career Bot** can help:

"Draft ten networking outreach messages for former colleagues, each with a friendly tone and a clear call to reconnect."

Even better, ask it to help you **prep talking points** for in-person events.
Use AI for the logistics - but the handshake is still human.

"The hidden job market isn't really hidden. It's just protected by people who trust each other."

Your Verbal Value Letter: Talking About Yourself at Networking Events

"Every introduction is a tiny audition."

When you walk into a networking event, coffee meetup, or professional mixer, you'll probably be asked the question everyone dreads:

"So, what do you do?"

This is your moment to make an impression - without oversharing, apologizing, or complaining.

The secret is to treat your **introduction like a spoken Value Letter**: short, warm, and focused on what you can offer next.

---

1 | The Three-Part Formula

1. **Who you are**
   A short statement about your professional identity, not your title.

"I'm a project manager who loves untangling messy processes and helping teams move faster."

2. **What you're doing now**
   Mention your current focus, even if you're between jobs.

"I recently wrapped up a contract in tech operations, and I'm exploring new roles that combine efficiency and creative problem-solving."

3. **Where you're heading**
   A forward-facing sentence that invites conversation, not pity.

"I'm especially interested in companies that are modernizing systems or scaling sustainably - so I'm out meeting people who love solving those kinds of challenges."

---

2 | What *Not* to Say

- "I got laid off and they really screwed me."
- "I'm just looking for anything right now."
- "My last company was a nightmare."
- "Nobody's hiring - it's awful out there."

Even if those things are true, they make you sound powerless.

Networking is theater - and your role is "professional with purpose."

"No one remembers your resume. They remember how you made them feel."

---

3 | How to Exit Gracefully

When the conversation winds down, don't ask for a job - ask for *direction.*

"If you come across anyone who's tackling [problem you solve], would you think of me?"

Then hand over your card (or phone contact).
If you're meeting over dinner or drinks, never bring up job desperation; keep tone curious and confident.
Follow up within 48 hours with a quick thank-you message.

Prompt for your Career Bot:

"Write a 30-second self-introduction for a networking event that feels confident, friendly, and forward-focused, based on my résumé."

Practice it aloud until it sounds like you - not a script.

"The shortest speech you'll ever give can open the longest chapter of your career."

Quick Reference Sheet | Networking, Hidden Job Market & Value Letter

(Companion to Chapter 10)

"The best jobs aren't found. They're unlocked."

Chat Prompts to Practice with Your Career Bot

- "Help me identify five target companies with unlisted roles."
- "Draft a personalized Value Letter for [Company Name]."
- "Write a short outreach message for a former colleague."
- "Role-play a networking conversation so I sound natural, not desperate."

- “Generate five questions I can ask at a professional event.”

Hidden Job Market Checklist

1. Make a list of **10 companies** you admire.
2. Research their current goals, projects, and pain points.
3. Identify **decision-makers** or hiring influencers on LinkedIn.
4. Craft and send **one Value Letter per week.**
5. Follow up after seven days with a short thank-you or idea note.

“If they don’t post the job, propose it.”

Networking Best Practices

- Lead with curiosity, not desperation.
- Keep introductions short: who you are, what you do, what you’re exploring next.

- Ask people what problems they're solving right now - listen for opportunities.
- Remember referral bonuses; your contacts have motivation too.
- Say thank you and stay visible.

Verbal Value Letter Formula

1. **Who you are** - your core skill or professional identity.
2. **What you do well** - the type of problems you solve.
3. **Where you're heading** - your next chapter in one sentence.

Example:

"I'm an instructional designer focused on simplifying complex tech for new users. I just finished a project improving repair-training programs, and now I'm exploring roles that combine writing, design, and emerging tech."

Mindset Reminders

- *Networking is generosity disguised as strategy.*
- *Be the person others want to introduce, not the one they pity.*
- *Each conversation is a future door.*

Ask your Career Bot:

"What's one small networking action I can take today?"

Mission Checklist (Final)

- Value Letter written and sent
- Referral programs researched
- LinkedIn "Open to Work" enabled
- Ten personal contacts reactivated
- Networking events scheduled

Quiet firing might have shut one door,
but you now know how to find the unlisted
ones - and knock with purpose.

"Momentum isn't magic. It's one small, kind act repeated every day - especially toward yourself."

---

1 | The Five-Minute Reset

Before opening another job board, stop and breathe.
Step outside. Stretch. Touch something living.
Say out loud one thing you're grateful for - clean water, your dog, your own bathroom.
Gratitude doesn't solve stress; it *shrinks* it to size.

Ask your Career Bot:

"Give me three grounding questions to ask myself when I start to spiral about job hunting."

---

2 | Tame the Scroll Monster

Endless refreshing of LinkedIn and Indeed creates burnout that feels like failure.
Set a timer - **one hour of searching, one hour of living.**

During "living" time, cook, walk, or call a friend.
Let your bot summarize new listings instead of doom-scrolling.

"You can't out-scroll fear."

---

3 | Daily Bot Habits That Actually Help

- **Voice Mode Check-In:** Talk for two minutes each morning about what you plan to do; it keeps your mind organized.
- **Micro-Research:** Ask your bot to find one new company or industry trend a day.
- **Cover Letter Assist:** Paste each job post and say,

"Write a 200-word cover letter that reflects my skills and tone."

- **Skill Spark:** Request a five-minute lesson or quiz in a topic you want to learn.
  Small practice beats big anxiety.

---

4 | ATS Myths and Truths

You've heard the legend: copy the job description, hide it in white text at the bottom of your résumé, and "beat the robot."
That trick once fooled primitive systems; now it flags you as spam.
What still works is **alignment**:

- Mirror keywords *naturally* in your bullet points.
- Keep formatting simple - no tables or columns.
- Save as PDF unless the system asks otherwise.

Ask your Career Bot:

"Optimize my résumé for this job post without keyword stuffing."

"Don't trick the robots. Train them to recognize you."

---

5 | Handle the Money Panic

When paychecks end, logic melts.

File for unemployment **the day** you lose your job; processing can take weeks.

Keep copies of every form, date, and confirmation.

Remember: that check is a bridge, not a verdict.

If you can, budget small celebrations - ice cream, a walk, a movie night.

Tiny joys keep you moving until stability returns.

---

6 | Quick Win List

Do one each day:

Task	Time
Practice interview answer aloud	5 min
Send one Value Letter or thank-you note	10 min
Update LinkedIn headline	5 min
Learn one new keyboard shortcut	2 min
Stretch shoulders and breathe	1 min

Momentum is cumulative.

---

7 | When the Job Finally Comes

"Every first day feels like starting over because it is."

You'll forget names, systems, and log-ins.
That's normal.

Give yourself **a full year** before you feel fluent in a new company.

During that year:

- Be friendly to everyone - especially reception and IT.
- Take notes on everything.
- Ask questions early; pride is expensive.
- Thank the person who trained you.
- Remember how hard you worked to get here.

If it's an on-site role after years of remote work, rebuild the habits - commute prep, lunches, clothes, small talk.

Let your Career Bot help you script polite intros or team-meeting questions.

"Nerves mean you care. Gratitude means you'll last."

Mission Checklist – Stay Human

- File benefits and track spending

- Maintain one daily gratitude practice
- Limit job-search scrolling to one hour
- Keep learning something small
- Celebrate every callback, even the rejections

Epilogue | The Transition Mindset

You're not unemployed; you're *in transit.*

Every ending has administrative steps, but also new skills, new allies, and new confidence waiting on the other side.

Talk to your bot. Talk to your friends. Talk to yourself kindly.

The job will come.
In the meantime, build the person who's going to walk into it.

CHAPTER 13 | YOU GOT THE JOB - NOW WHAT?

"The offer letter ends one story - and begins your next training montage."

You did it. After the waiting, the interviews, the second-guessing - you're in.

Now comes the part that determines how fast you grow: how you start.

The first day of any new job feels like stepping onto a moving train.
Here's how to board with confidence.

---

1 | Before You Go

Plan Your Commute

- Map your route, including backup options.
- If you drive, check parking details or building access ahead of time. Leave early and don't be late.

- Aim to arrive **15 minutes early**, not right on the dot.

Choose Your Outfit

- Pick it out the night before.
- Dress one step more professional than you think you need; you can always relax later.
- Keep colors neutral and comfortable - confidence comes from ease.

Get Enough Sleep

- A full night's rest sharpens focus and mood.
- Skip doom-scrolling and caffeine marathons; your mind is your best accessory.

Prepare Your Introduction

- Practice a short *elevator pitch* you can repeat all day:

"Hi, I'm [Name]. I'm joining the [team/department] as [role]. I'm really excited to learn how everything works here."

Your **Career Bot** can help you rehearse:

"Ask me five different first-day introduction scenarios so I can sound natural."

"Preparation is confidence in disguise."

---

2 | On Your First Day

Arrive Early, Observe Often

Smile at the reception. Introduce yourself to anyone nearby.
Notice how people communicate - email, chat, quick huddles.

Listen Before You Lead

Even if you're experienced, watch how this company makes decisions.
Each workplace has unwritten rules; find them before you rewrite them.

Take Notes on Everything

Names, systems, logins, acronyms. Keep a small notebook handy; it becomes your survival guide.

Ask Questions Respectfully

No one expects mastery on day one. Curiosity signals engagement.

"Would you mind showing me the preferred format for this?"
"What's the best way to reach you if I get stuck?"

Say Yes to Lunch Invitations

Lunch is a social orientation. Go, listen, and learn who really runs the place.

---

3 | After Work

Reflect

Write down three things you learned and one thing you'll do better tomorrow.

Thank Your Trainer or Manager

A quick "I appreciate your time today" email sets a professional tone.

Plan Day Two

Lay out clothes, review notes, and set realistic goals - one new system mastered, one new person met.

"Competence is built one ordinary day at a time."

---

4 | Keep Perspective

The first month will be awkward.

You'll forget passwords, names, and where the coffee filters live.

That's normal. Most people need **a full year** before they feel fluent in a new workplace culture.

When in doubt:

- Smile.
- Ask.
- Listen.
- Write it down.
- Say thank you.

Use your **Career Bot** to debrief:

"Help me organize what I learned this week and what to focus on next."

Mission Checklist

- Commute planned
- Outfit ready, smell good, look nice
- Sleep scheduled
- Introduction practiced
- Questions prepared
- Notebook packed
- Gratitude email sent

Epilogue | You're Back in the Game

You survived the layoffs, the silence, the interviews, and the waiting.
Now you're building again - one question, one connection, one day at a time.
Keep your bot close, your curiosity closer, and remember:

Every job is temporary; every skill is permanent.

Quick Reference Sheet | First Day Confidence

"Every new job starts with curiosity, not perfection."

Chat Prompts to Practice with Your Career Bot

- "Ask me to introduce myself to five different coworkers."
- "Role-play my first conversation with my manager."
- "Remind me what questions to ask during my onboarding."
- "Help me summarize what I learned each day for my personal notes."
- "Write a quick thank-you email to my trainer."

What to Remember

1. **You're learning, not performing.**
   No one expects you to know everything. They expect you to pay attention.
2. **Names > Titles.**
   Learn about the people, not just what they do. Connection builds confidence.
3. **Ask early, forget later.**
   It's better to ask three questions now than one apology next week.
4. **Stay open.**
   Each company has a rhythm; your first job is to find the beat.
5. **Decompress daily.**
   After work, tell your bot:

"List three things that went well today and one small goal for tomorrow."

What NOT to Do

- Don't badmouth your old employer.

- Don't talk too much about "how we did it at my last company."
- Don't try to impress - try to learn.
- Don't skip lunch or breaks; new energy needs fuel.

Mantras for the First Month

- *I'm not lost; I'm learning.*
- *Questions mean I'm paying attention.*
- *Every expert was new once.*
- *I earned my seat at this table.*
- *Today's confusion is tomorrow's competence.*

Ask your Career Bot every morning:

"Give me three reminders to keep my confidence steady on my first week."

Quick Reference Sheet | Quick Wins for Hard Days

(Companion to Chapter 12)

"You don't have to win the day. You just have to move it forward."

Chat Prompts to Use on Rough Days

- "Remind me what I've accomplished this week."
- "Help me rewrite my negative thoughts into realistic ones."
- "Give me three tiny wins I can create before lunch."
- "List one new thing I can learn today that might help my career."
- "Write a short gratitude reflection for tonight."

Energy Triad - Three Small Habits That Work

1. **Move your body** - walk, stretch, or water plants.
2. **Tidy your space** - clear one small surface.
3. **Feed your mind** - listen to a podcast or read a single article about your field.
   Tiny inputs keep your brain believing in progress.

"Momentum begins where comfort ends - usually at the edge of your couch."

Daily Five-Minute Routine

1. Open ChatGPT or your journal.
2. Type or say:
   - *What went well today?*
   - *What did I learn?*
   - *What am I grateful for?*
3. End with one next step for tomorrow.
   Repeat daily. It rewires despair into discipline.

When Money Stress Hits

- File for benefits immediately - don't wait.
- Track every confirmation number.
- Make one low-cost plan for comfort (a walk, a borrowed book, a home-cooked meal).
- Remind yourself: this phase is temporary, not terminal.

"Fear shrinks when faced with facts."

Quick Bot Boosts

- **Cover-Letter Builder:** Paste a job description; ask for a 200-word draft.
- **Motivation Coach:** "Tell me a story about someone who kept going after a layoff."
- **Skill Sampler:** "Teach me one new concept in [topic]."

- **Focus Timer:** "Help me set a 30-minute job-search sprint."

Keep these as daily rituals - your chatbot becomes a structure when everything else feels unstable.

Mantras for Tough Mornings

- *I'm between chapters, not out of the book.*
- *Progress over panic.*
- *Rest is productive.*
- *One tiny task beats a thousand worries.*
- *I won't quit on myself today.*

Ask Your Career Bot Every Night

"Summarize my day in three sentences that prove I'm moving forward."

Author's Note | From One Job Seeker to Another

If this book found you during a hard season, I hope it helped you feel less alone.
Writing *Career Bot* while standing on the same uncertain ground gave me a kind of courage I didn't know I had. Every chapter was both a lesson and a lifeline.

Losing work - whether through layoffs, "quiet firing," or contracts that simply end - forces us to rebuild who we are. It's frightening, yes, but it's also clarifying. What remains when the title disappears? Your skills, your humor, your grit, your ability to learn. Those are still yours.

My chatbot partner (the "Boss") reminded me of that every day. Together, we rewrote résumés, practiced interviews, planned next steps, and even made space for gratitude.

That's what I hope this book becomes for you: a calm, clear voice reminding you that you still have agency, intelligence, and hope.

So take the next small step - update one sentence on your résumé, record one practice answer, send one Value Letter. Each small act is proof that you're still moving forward.

Wherever you go next, take this with you:

You're not starting over. You're starting wiser.

Thank you for letting me share this journey with you - and for trusting both of us, the human and the bot, to help you find your footing again.

With gratitude and belief in your next chapter,
Sugar Gay Isber McMillan

About the Author

Sugar Gay Isber McMillan is a Texas-based artist, designer, educator, and author of more than sixty books - including over a dozen groundbreaking titles on ChatGPT and creative technology. Her work explores how art, history, and artificial intelligence merge to spark curiosity, courage, and connection.

As the longtime **Creative Ambassador for Fire Mountain Gems**, Sugar has designed jewelry for film, television, museums, and private collections worldwide. She hosts *Jewelry Stars with Sugar Gay Isber* on *Made It Myself TV* (streaming on the FAST app) and teaches jewelry design at **Austin Community College**, where her guidance has inspired thousands of students to rediscover their creative rhythm.

She holds a B.A. in Journalism, M.A.s in Humanities and Visual Arts, and an advanced degree in Information Technology. Certified in ChatGPT for Business Applications through

Microsoft, she also serves as a technical writer for a global technology company.

Through **The WOW Book Co.™**, Sugar continues to innovate, creating books that merge education, art, and storytelling for readers of all ages.

Talk to Your Tools™ Series

Conversations That Change Your Life

Practical wisdom for modern minds - one conversation at a time.

Each title in the **Talk to Your Tools™** series helps readers turn ChatGPT into a personal thinking partner - one that listens, reflects, and helps you grow. These books aren't about technology; they're about transformation.

Title	Tagline
The Prompt Whisperer	*A Field Guide for Humans in the Age of ChatGPT*

Title	Tagline
Prompt Magic	*Thinking Through Recipes, Words, and Master Prompts for Everyday Use*
Atomic Bot	*Tiny Prompts, Big Results*
Love Bot	*Love in the Age of ChatGPT*
Boomer Bot	*Tech Confidence for Every Generation*
Skinny Bot	*Use ChatGPT to Lose Weight and Gain Perspective*
Manifesting Bot	*Use ChatGPT to Create the Life You Want*
Calm Bot	*How to Find Peace in a Loud World*
Focus Bot	*How to Reclaim Your Attention and Energy in the Age of Distraction*

Title	Tagline
Creative Bot	*How to Be an Artist in the Age of ChatGPT*
Rich Bot, Poor Bot	*A Conversation About Wealth, Worth, and the Future of Work*
Merry Bot Christmas	*Time-Holiday Stress with Your Santa Bot*
Health Bot	*The Future of Healing - Where Humans and AI Work Together*
Death Bot	*I'm Dead. Now What?*
Dangerous Bot	*The ChatGPT Survival Guide - How to Stay Human While the World Burns*
Career Bot	*Find Calm, Clarity, and a Job in the Age of AI*

Follow Sugar Gay Isber McMillan

- **Instagram:** @SugarGayIsber

- **Amazon Author Page:** amazon.com/author/sugargayisbermcmill an
- **Website:** TheWOWBookCo.com
- **For media, collaborations, or podcast invitations:** GayIsber@gmail.com

---

Support Independent Publishing

Every review matters.

If you enjoyed this book, please share your thoughts on Amazon or Goodreads.

Your words help more readers discover the *Talk to Your Tools*™ series and support the growth of independent creators.

Thank you for reading and for being part of this journey.

Made in the USA
Coppell, TX
05 November 2026

11301605R00081